POW:
PROMISES KEPT

To all my dear friends
at Boone County
Library — thanks.
You for your dedication
to all who
turn to you;
—very LIFE—
Itself
In Words

"Boots" Mayberry

POW: Promises Kept
The Inspiring Stories of Walter Boots Mayberry
Copyright © 2014 by Linda Apple

All photos from the collection of Walter Mayberry.

This is a work of nonfiction. All details are accurate to the best of the subject's memory.

First Edition
Printed and bound in the United States

ISBN: 978-1-940222-99-8

Cover design by Kelsey Rice
Formatting by Kelsey Rice

POW:
PROMISES KEPT

The Inspiring Stories of Walter "Boots" Mayberry

AS TOLD TO Linda Apple

P
Pen-L Publishing
Fayetteville, AR
Pen-L.com

DEDICATION

I dedicate this book to my departed wife, Marion, who listened to these stories patiently through the sixty-two years of our marriage. It is not easy to live with a former Prisoner of War but she did, with love and grace.

She was one who waited and prayed for someone she knew not then, but one who was to appear soon in her life.

It is not my intention to derogate my former enemies of so many years ago. I have been reconciled to them, and thank them for being a pivotal point in my Christian lifestyle and thinking.

CONTENTS

BOOTS MARCHING ONWARD

PREFACE

By Linda Apple

I met Boots a few months before his ninetieth birthday and had the pleasure of hearing about his incredible life. While listening to him I knew his experiences must be written down and shared.

When I first conceived this memoir I decided to focus on Boots's service during World War II. But after hearing stories about his childhood, I realized how well growing up during the Great Depression had prepared him and young men like him for World War II. Not only that, his being held prisoner by the German army had formed the man he is today and clarified his purpose. Therefore, I divided the book into three sections: his childhood, his war years, and his life after he returned. I've also included several poems from his book, *A Distant Drummer,* to give a glimpse into his soul as only poetry can.

Boots asked that I not be graphic about his experience as a prisoner of war, stating that it opens old wounds. I have honored his request, but as you read about his capture and time spent in prison camp it is important to realize the inconceivable pain, trauma, and dread he experienced. And yet, he not only survived but he has grown into a wise, faith-filled man as a result. He did not allow the pain, discouragement, or fear defeat him.

As Boots puts it, "I try to not look back. Yesterday is past. You cannot do anything about it. Tomorrow is not yours, it belongs to the Lord. Today is the only one your can do anything about. Help someone."

Helping others is what this book is about.

Boots also asked that I not portray him as a hero. I must confess that is hard to do because I consider him a hero, as I do all who spend their lives in the service for others.

It is both Boots's and my prayer that you will find hope, encouragement, and strength as you read *POW: Promises Kept, The Inspiring Stories of Walter Boots Mayberry.*

INTRODUCTION

Even in darkness light dawns for the upright, for those who are gracious and compassionate and righteous. ~ Psalm 112:4

A huge black cloud of metallic splinters burst under the bomber and caused it to rock. Holes were blown through the aluminum fuselage. Two bursts hit close. The third hit the in-board engine on the right wing and it caught fire.

When Boots bailed out, he couldn't tell where he was in relation to the ground and didn't realize he was falling head first with his feet up. When he pulled the ripcord it jerked him around with such force two vertebrae in his neck broke. He lost the use of his hands and he couldn't guide his parachute. Boots floated helplessly to earth under a thirty-foot silk canopy.

All around him was a cacophony of anti-aircraft fire. Shrapnel and wreckage from destroyed airplanes hurtled past him. Fear and dread filled his mind. *What if this wreckage hit him or his parachute and dragged him down to certain death?* In the deafening noise of all this melee, he cried out, "God, help me."

In the 1940's, life's path filled with promise for most young men. Some went to college, others began a trade. Some fell in love and married, others played the field. All looked to a bright promising future.

Some, but not all.

Walter "Boots" Mayberry, a member of the Army Air Corps, felt he had no promise of a future. At twenty-one he was already an old man. Due to injuries he sustained when his airplane was shot down, malnutrition, and exposure, he lay in a building where the guards moved captives who were dying in order to get them out of the way. Death waited at Boot's door and frankly, he no longer cared. It would have been an escape from the German prison camp, Stalag Luft #13 in Nuremberg, where he wasted away as a prisoner of war.

But there was a promise waiting for him.

One evening a guard stepped through the door and said, "The American troops have advanced. We are moving to Moosburg. All who can fall out do so. If not, we will leave you here to die."

That one last spark of the will to live fired in Boots. He rolled onto his hands and knees and crawled toward the door when he noticed through the dim, dusky light, something on the floor. Curious, he inched toward it and found a New Testament and Psalms bible. It was opened to Psalms 91. He couldn't see very well, so he squinted and bent closer. The words he read were a promise from God.

> *Whoever dwells in the shelter of the Most High* will rest in the shadow of the Almighty
>
> *I will say of the Lord, "He is my refuge and my fortress, my God, in whom I trust."*
>
> *Surely he will save you from the fowler's snare and from the deadly pestilence.*
>
> *He will cover you with his feathers, and under his wings you will find refuge; his faithfulness will be your shield and rampart.*
>
> *You will not fear the terror of night, nor the arrow that flies by day, nor the pestilence that stalks in the darkness, nor the plague that destroys at midday.*

A thousand may fall at your side, ten thousand at your right hand, but it will not come near you. You will only observe with your eyes and see the punishment of the wicked.

If you say, "The Lord is my refuge," and you make the Most High your dwelling, no harm will overtake you, no disaster will come near your tent. For he will command his angels concerning you to guard you in all your ways; they will lift you up in their hands, so that you will not strike your foot against a stone. You will tread on the lion and the cobra; you will trample the great lion and the serpent. "Because he loves me," says the Lord, "I will rescue him; I will protect him, for he acknowledges my name. He will call on me, and I will answer him; I will be with him in trouble, I will deliver him and honor him. With long life I will satisfy him and show him my salvation."

Boots hadn't given God much thought, but in the dank gloom, he knew he had heard from Heaven. These words gave him the strength to go on, to walk out of the door of death with renewed hope. God had something for him to do and promised him a long life in which to do it.

Boots celebrated his 91st birthday in August of 2014. God has indeed given Boots a long life for a purpose—to share the love of Christ and to keep the promises he has made throughout his life.

For those imprisoned souls, those who are ready to give up, and those who feel there is no hope, this book is for you.

It is a reminder that even in darkness, light dawns.

BOOTS

MY NAME IS BOOTS MAYBERRY

On August 11, 1923, Walter Morris Mayberry struggled his way into the world, fighting for his life. He didn't enter the new world the way most children do, head first. He met the world bottom first, a breech birth.

His exhausted mother, Edith, and anxious father, Walter, for whom he was named, welcomed their new son into the family home on East Sixth Street in Pine Bluff, Arkansas. He was their fourth child. His difficult birth left him a sickly child. However, he soldiered on and overcame the odds, as he would do all through his life.

Little Walter began life in the bustling love of a large family. In addition to his mother, father, older brother, and two older sisters, his grandparents also lived in the house on East Sixth Street—a very special Colonial-style house. His mother believed it was haunted. He remembers his Grandfather Richter telling about being woken in the night by something pulling his toe, though no one and nothing else was around. His mother also told of dishes falling off the mantelpiece in the night. Though proof of ghosts' existence was never actually proven, the family accepted their presence in the home.

The Great Flood of 1927 was the catalyst for Little Walter's nickname "Boots." The warm weather that year led to an early snowmelt in Canada that caused the upper Mississippi River to swell. The upper

Boots, age 6

Midwest had an unusually wet spring sending full rivers rushing into the Mississippi. Both of those events, combined with the excessive rain in Arkansas, made the Mississippi and Arkansas rivers and all the tributaries overflow their banks. It was the most destructive flood in Arkansas history, to human and animal life as well as financially.

Walter was four at the time. He remembers lying on his front porch dangling his fingers in the brown, muddy water as it flowed by his house on the east side of Pine Bluff. One afternoon his sister, Dell, took him to town and bought him a pair of rubber boots with a red-rimmed tops. Excitedly, he put them on and splashed about. From that point on he never wanted to take them off, not even to bathe or go to bed. Even if he didn't have anything else on, he always wore his rubber red-tops. Therefore, Dell started calling him Boots.

The name became official when he started first grade at Sixth Avenue School. His teacher, Miss Ovida Sanders, asked his name and he replied, "Boots Mayberry."

And so it has been ever since.

THE BEST OF TIMES, THE WORST OF TIMES...

Boots uses Dickens's famous quote to describe growing up during the Great Depression. It was the worst of times for his parents who labored to provide for their large family. His father worked seven days a week. He never took a vacation because he was afraid to leave his job. During the Great Depression years, if a person took time off his job, someone else might have it when he returned. His mother fed the family from their large garden on the corner lot by their house.

And yet, as hard as those times were, he remembers his childhood as being the best of times. After the flood his father moved the family to 315 Beech Street near Trinity Episcopal Church. Pine Bluff had two railroads serving the area at that time. They moved to a house one block away from two sets of tracks. On the North side of the house the Cotton Belt ran; on the South ran the Missouri Pacific. Boots enjoyed watching the big steam engines roar by and getting the engineers to blow the whistle when they saw him. His dad made good use of the train as well. Each morning he'd run and jump on the caboose to go to work in town.

Boots's family was a railroad family. When his parents married, his father worked for the Railway Express Agency in Newport, Arkansas. His uncle Alf, a conductor for the Cotton Belt, rode in the caboose. Boots and his siblings always waited for him to pass by to wave at him.

Uncle Eighme was the engineer on the Lone Star Limited, a fast passenger train that ran between Dallas and Memphis. This big steam engine would pass through Pine Bluff at three a.m. and ornery Uncle Eighme never failed to blow the whistle when he passed by the Mayberry home, waking all in the house.

Things were tight economically, but Boots had no idea they were poor. He and his friends didn't have a lot of store-bought toys. Who needed them? Discarded apple cart crates made great scooters when skate wheels were attached. Broken crates provided wood to whittle airplanes and other toys. The trash behind the Kress Five and Dime store provided a bounty of broken toys for the boys to use in their clubhouse.

Anything to do with writing fascinated Boots. Sometimes while digging through the dime store discards he sometimes found a treasure trove of pencils and tablets. He loved to read too. He got his first library card when he was ten years old. He liked the feel of the paper pages and the smell of newsprint. His reading tastes varied. He enjoyed fiction, especially Western and detective stories, non-fiction, classics and poetry. Another favorite was anything about aviation, something he'd come to know a lot about as an adult.

Boots was also rich in friends. His first friend was Wesley Price. They enjoyed going to the movies, especially the ones with cowboys. Hopalong Cassidy and the Texas Rangers sparked their imaginations and many an evening was spent playing cowboys and Indians.

One special memory was the club he and his friends had formed, the Junior G-Men club, inspired by a children's radio program by the same name and hosted by Melvin Purvis. As part of the radio program, listeners could request and receive badges, manuals, and secret agent props.

During this period of time, Hot Springs, Arkansas, was neutral ground—an open city—for outlaws such as Al Capone and Bonnie and Clyde, who came there for the races and the hot mineral baths. They

Ready to go after the bad guys!

had an agreement with the city government: *When we come here, we won't bother you and you won't bother us.* Consequently, all of these outlaws were in Pine Bluff at one time or another and Boots's father saw them all.

Being faithful Junior G-Men, the boys often climbed high in their clubhouse and watched the trains, hoping to see one of these famous criminals and help capture them, thus becoming heroes and receiving a large reward!

Little did he know then, but one day he would become a hero to everyone but himself.

THE WORLD COMES TO BOOTS

Growing up in Pine Bluff in the '30s and '40s offered Boots a wealth of culture and experiences. Until he enlisted, he'd never traveled more than a few miles from his hometown, but that didn't keep him from international influences.

Large German, Jewish, Italian, and Chinese communities called Pine Bluff home. There was also a large Jewish Synagogue, the Anshe Emeth (Men of Truth) chartered in 1867. The synagogue has since been sold in 2003 to a local hospital and has been converted to a nursing school.

Each community had their own neighborhood grocery store. Close to Boots's home was a Chinese market. His family bought groceries there on credit during the week with the promise of paying on Saturday. He still remembers going with his father to settle the week's account. Mr. Hing always gave him *lagniappe,* a small gift given with a purchase or in this case, a little treat given for the payment, usually piece of candy. This was the practice at most of the markets. They were grateful to be paid during the depression when so many couldn't pay.

As a child, Boots learned that people were different in appearance and speech. He also learned about their holidays and how they were celebrated. Because his father was a policeman, these communities often gave his father gifts of food from their celebrations and Boots was introduced to matzo ball soup and other unusual cuisine.

Yes, the world had come to Boots as a child, but in a few short years he would be sent out to the world as an adult.

MUSIC AND FOLKS

Behind Boots's house was a row of four shacks his father rented to the local black folks who came to the town for work. Most worked for wealthy families in town, cooking and cleaning for them. Some took in washing. They built a fire under a large black pot outside their shack to soak and boil the clothing. Others worked for local businesses like a fellow named George, who drove the ice wagon and delivered frozen blocks to homes for the iceboxes. As he rode down the street he'd call out, "Iiiiiice man!" Homemakers had cards that indicated how many pounds they wanted and when they heard his call they would hurry out and put their cards on the front porch. George would then chip out their order, carry it in the house and put it in the box.

The kids were especially excited to hear George's call because of the *snow dust* he had under a burlap bag in the back of his wagon. Snow dust was made when the large blocks of ice at the icehouse were scored for easier chilling and breaking apart. George would gather it up for the children he'd meet along the way and give them a snowball. One could say these ancestors of today's snow cones were George's form of lagniappe.

When Boots was a boy, aviation was in its infancy. Barnstorming where stunt pilots performed death-defying tricks became a popular form of entertainment. Some pilots also sold airplane rides. Wooden toy airplanes became all the rage. The kids whittled airplanes out of blocks of wood and carved propellers from the slats of wooden crates. The propellers turned like windmills when attached to the toy plane. This caught George's eye and he had an idea. One day while the kids waited for their snow, he turned to Boots and said, "Mr. Boots, would you whittle me out one of those propellers? I want to put it on my ice wagon." Boots said he would one of these days, but time passed, Boots entered his teenage years, graduated, and went to war. The idea was forgotten—well, to everyone except George.

After the war Boots walked down Main Street and saw an elderly black man with a pushcart that read *Hot Tamales 25 cents a dozen*. When the man saw Boots he broke out in a smile. It was George. The first thing George said to Boots was, "Mr. Boots. You never made me that propeller." Boots said, "No George. I never did. But while I was dropping bombs over Germany, I'd sometimes say, 'Here's one for my friend George.'"

George smiled and said, "That's even better." To this day George holds a special place in Boots's heart.

There was one man, a former opera singer by the name of Bob Kastor, who worked as a ticket collector at the theater, which was once the opera house. The Saenger Theater, called *The Showplace of the South,* was one of the three hundred such theaters the Saenger brothers built during the 1920s. The opulent deco design was spacious with cathedral glass ceilings and chandeliers.

In keeping with the dramatic operatic influence, Mr. Kastor dressed in costume and wore theater make-up. His stately and intimidating appearance scared the kids spitless.

The price of a ticket for kids was ten cents until they were thirteen, when the price increased to twenty-five cents. When Boots turned thirteen, he still told Mr. Kastor he was twelve. Sometimes he had to stop a block away and refigure the year he'd been born to prove he was twelve since the man always asked. Every time Mr. Kastor asked, "Boy, how old are you? What year were you born?" To which Boots replied he was twelve and gave the year that would prove him to be that age. This became a game with them.

Once when Boots was home on leave from the service, Mr. Kastor walked up to him and said, "Boots, I see with your uniform and medals that you finally got to be thirteen."

The love of music took hold of Boots as a young boy, especially the blues. Boots ascribes his budding love of music in part to Leo and Lilly, a couple who lived in one of the shacks at the back of his house. Leo was a blues singer and guitarist. Boots visited them often and listened to Leo sing and play while Lilly made Johnnycakes. He remembers being fascinated with the walls of the shack. They were covered with the comics from the newspaper. Each week Leo mixed up a paste of flour and water and covered the walls. He told Boots this gave him something to look at and it helped to keep the cabin warm.

Appreciation for music continued to grow in seven-year-old Boots. He became interested in the drums as a young boy. The First World War had ended eleven years earlier and there were still a lot of military parades. The 4th of July celebrations always included marching bands. Many Civil War veterans were still alive then. The drums in these bands fascinated Boots.

Once, after seeing Bob Wills and the Light Crust Doughboys—later to become the Texas Playboys—at the Alamo Theater, he went home and gathered up some cardboard boxes. Then he found some tree twigs for drumsticks and started playing. For Christmas his sister bought him a toy drum. Finally, he had the real deal. He began teaching himself how to beat out the rhythm while listening to music on the radio. Fortunately, the high school band director, Mr. Scrubby Watson, believed in developing music appreciation and interest in children at a

Boots, in the band

very young age, so he began a music program for elementary students. Boots took free drum lessons from Fred Schneider, a drummer in Mr. Watson's band. He stuck with it and when he entered Woodrow Wilson Junior High he signed up for band. He played in the Pine Bluff High School Band until he left for service in 1943.

To this day Boots describes himself as one who hears a different drummer. One who must, as written about in Henry David Thoreau's *Conclusion*, "*Let him* step to the music which he hears, however measured or far away."

OFFICER DUCK MAYBERRY

The Quiet Man

Boots comes from a heritage of law enforcers. His grandfather and uncle both served as deputy sheriffs and both were killed in the line of duty. His father, Walter, left the railroad and became a member of the Pine Bluff police department in 1919. He retired in 1943.

His father's nickname, *Duck*, given to him as a youngster because he raised ducks, was a paradox of sorts. Officer Duck Mayberry had a reputation of being a fair but rugged policeman—a person one wouldn't want to cross. He walked the nightwatch beat in the roughest part of town, near the railroad tracks where hobos and tramps jumped off the trains to beg or steal a meal.

Once a hobo decided he'd do away with Duck Mayberry. He jumped off the train with a lead pipe hidden in a gunnysack. But he didn't know the Mayberry's were a rugged breed. The poor guy took a whipping and ended up in jail, licking his wounds.

Boots's father worked hard to support the family, seven days a week, all night long. Therefore he slept during the day, leaving very little time for outings. Boots recalls his father never talked much. He was a quiet man. But he always showed that he cared.

Even though his father worked hard at nights and slept during the days, as Boots looks back, he did enjoy special times with his father on the occasional fishing or hunting trip.

Boots's dad, Walter "Duck" Mayberry

They lived close to a prison near Cummings, Arkansas. Their house had footings on brick blocks and it was easy to see all the way underneath it. One winter several prisoners escaped from Cummings. The posse and their bloodhounds, the police and prison guards, went in search of the escapees. The bloodhounds lead them straight to Duck Mayberry's house, barking to beat the band. Boots and the family heard all the commotion, dogs howling and people shouting. They wondered what was going on and looked out the door in time to see prisoners fleeing in every direction from underneath the house where they had been hiding, with the cops and dogs in hot pursuit behind them. Boots laughed and said, "It looked like one of those old Keystone Cops movies."

That house had another notorious aspect. Before Boots's family moved in, a bootlegger had lived there. Prohibition was in effect at that time. It wasn't uncommon to have a caller knocking at Officer Mayberry's door during all hours of the night wanting a little moonshine. Imagine their surprise when they realized whose home they were calling on.

Since Duck was a policeman, he often found himself the object of a lot of practical jokes. One time someone stole a car and parked it in the Mayberry driveway. Officers searched all over for the missing automobile. It was rather embarrassing for it to be discovered in the front yard of a patrolman from the Pine Bluff police department.

History seemed to repeat itself when Boots was thirteen. One evening he decided to see a movie. He left the house after supper around six-thirty and headed toward the Sanger Theater, which was about six blocks up on West 2nd Avenue. He'd gotten about halfway there when he heard his mother call, "Boots."

He turned around and hurried back home. When got there he asked his mother why she called for him. She looked at him with a worried frown and said, "I didn't call you." Then she told him his dad had been shot.

While answering a domestic disturbance call, Duck had walked onto the yard to see what was going on. Without warning, the man who lived there stuck a shotgun around the corner of the house and shot him with a load of number eight bird shot just above the heart.

In the hospital the surgeon tried to remove all the lead shot, but couldn't remove all the pellets without endangering his heart. It is believed the lead leached into Duck's body and the poison eventually weakened him. After that incident Duck's health deteriorated over the following ten years and he had to retire from the police department.

Walter Duck Mayberry passed away in 1948. Like his grandfather and uncle, he was injured in the line of duty. The future held the same fate for Walter Boots Mayberry.

EDITH MAYBERRY

The Heart Of The Home

Boots's mother, Edith Catherine Richter, was a woman of strong character and Christian faith. She believed in herself and did what had to be done with a determined focus—a good thing to have in those hard times.

She was a lovely woman with especially beautiful eyes. Although she jokingly told Boots that while she was bringing him into the world, he nearly took her out of it. Truth be known, she loved him dearly and was very possessive of him, especially when he got an eye for girls.

Being a stay-at-home mom was the norm in those days. And these moms worked hard. Edith cooked for her large family from the garden. Meals consisted of beans, potatoes, soups and a lot of turnip greens. And even if there wasn't a lot of variety in the meals, it was served with love and the family enjoyed it together around the table. Boots points out that no meal started until everyone was there.

It is a good thing this remarkable woman had a stout heart. Since her husband slept during the day and worked during the night, it was up to Edith to corral her rambunctious boys. More than once they gave her reason to grab her broom, chase them down and lay a few licks on them.

Boots's mom, Edith

One such time was when Tom Mix, a western movie star at the time, came to town and put on a shooting performance on stage. Eleven-year-old Boots and his sixteen-year-old brother Edward, whom he called Bud, went to see Tom's show. Mix dazzled them with his tricks, using blank bullets, of course.

After the show Boots and Bud went to the stage door and waited to meet Mix. When Mix came to the door, the brothers asked him for a souvenir. The cowboy reached in his pocket and gave them a handful of shells. Boots didn't know what they were, but Bud did.

The boys' dad had the same caliber pistol, a large .45 silver-plated revolver, that he brought home each morning and emptied it of bullets before he went to bed. Bud took the gun and the boys went outside to the part of their yard where there were no other houses around. Bud loaded the blank shells, handed it to Boots and said, "Boots, why don't you shoot the gun? Won't nothing happen."

Boots replied, "Why don't you shoot it?"

"No," said Bud. "I want you to shoot it."

Boots put both hands on the handle, still unsure.

"Go ahead," urged Bud. "Pull the trigger. Won't nothing happen. It won't make any noise. I just want to see if you can shoot it."

So Boots used all his strength to pull the trigger. Finally he succeeded and BOOM! He threw the gun down and shouted triumphantly, "I shot it! I shot it!"

His mom was alone in the kitchen, sweeping, when she heard the blast—followed by what she thought was Boots shouting, "I shot him, I shot him." Filled with panic, broom still in hand, it took her two tries to get outside because the broom was crossways when she hit the door.

When she finally got outside she found Bud holding his sides, laughing. She froze, taking it all in. When she realized what had happened, that Bud had tricked his brother, she charged at him with the broom. He took off running with her close behind.

His father slept on, never stirring. It was when things got too quiet that he woke up.

As mentioned earlier, Edith was a woman of strong Christian values. She believed in feeding the poor. Word got out among the hobos, tramps, and homeless that Edith Mayberry would give gifts of food. Boots never knew her to turn anyone away, even though there were many mouths to feed at home.

In just a few short years, her bravery and compassion would be called upon once again when her rowdy boys became young soldiers.

BROTHERS & SISTERS ~ THE MAYBERRY DYNASTY

Boots was the fourth child in the line of Mayberry siblings. His two sisters, Violet Virginia, nicknamed *Violent Virginia* by her siblings, and Edith Ardell, nicknamed *Dell,* were the first two children of Walter and Edith. Then came Edward (Bud), then Boots, then Jack Randall.

Virginia had a good steady mind and she was a hard worker. Her temperament wasn't an affectionate one, however. She just didn't seem to know how to exhibit love.

Dell was just the opposite. She had a loving spirit, a beautiful nature, kind and gentle. She willingly gave whatever she had to share.

Bud was handsome and athletic, liked by all the girls. And he was a good student.

Ten years after Boots, Jack was born. Boots took his little brother under his wing and Jack always looked up to him. At the time of this writing, Boots and Jack are the only surviving members of the family.

After hearing Boots's tales about how he and Bud had tormented their sisters, I can understand why Violet was sometimes dubbed Violent. The little brothers seemed to make it their mission to ensure that their sisters would be old maids.

They always popped up somewhere when their sisters were with their boyfriends. Violet and Dell often invited young men to the house

Boots with his brothers and sisters

to dance. They'd wind up the Victrola and play music in hopes the boys would do the Dipsy Doodle with them.

Bud and Boots would hang around until their sisters chased them away. However, the brothers had another trick up their sleeve, so to speak. They would go to the back room and fire up their electric toy train set with all its bells and whistles. In no time Virginia and Dell's dates would leave them, go to the back room and fall on the floor to play with the little brothers.

Some things, like the dynamics between brothers and sisters, never change.

PATHWAYS

by Boots Mayberry

When I was six, my mother took me by the hand and said,
"It is time for you to go, my boy."
Off we went to Sixth Avenue Elementary.
My eyes followed her all the way across and out of the room.
A small, feeble wave of my hand lifted from my new desk,
left her with eyes that glistened as the door closed behind her,
for I was hers alone no longer, nor she mine.
I had started my lonely walk into a new age.

When I was eighteen, I took my mother by the hand and said,
"It is time for me to go, my mother."
War had come to the world and families were broken apart
never to be the same.
My eyes glistened as I left her, for I was hers alone no longer, nor she mine.
I had started my solitary walk into the world
of man's inhumanity to man.

When I was twenty-six, I took my mother by the hand and said,
"It is time for me to go, my mother."
I went off with a tear and a smile with someone new

who had found a place in my heart.
I was hers alone no longer, nor she mine.
We had started our new walk along a different pathway together.

When I was fifty-seven, my mother said to me,
"It is time for me to go, my son."
Her eyes followed me all the way across and out of the room.
From her white bed draped with tubes and bottles
a small, frail hand lifted and gave a weak wave
as I left her for the last time.
She was mine alone no longer, nor I hers.
She had begun her solitary walk
into the ages.

Boots and his mom

315 BEECH

by Boots Mayberry

The front door hangs askew on its hinges
as if welcoming company into the lonely house.
The rain slants down outside and the clouds hang low and heavy,
obscuring the sunlight and filling the front room with a dark, grey mist.

I push open the door gingerly and speak in a monotone
that falls on unhearing walls, "Is anybody home?"
I receive naught except the sound of the rain falling into dead leaves
that have blown up in drifts around the front porch.

As I step into the grey of the front room my vision is directed
to the fireplace, surrounded by battered furniture.
Couches with tufts of cotton bursting forth from their covering.
Chairs with springs exploding from their interior.

The mantelpiece lined with a mixture of old beer cans and whiskey bottles
Left in some last celebration or fit of despondency.
As I step farther into the interior
The gloom is suddenly lifted.

The fireplace is transformed with a warm, entrancing glow
once more decorated with garlands of holly and ivy.
Sparkling candles gleam and tinsel reflects
Back its golden glints.

In the corner where dust and cobwebs hang suddenly appears the
Christmas pine in all its glory. Strings of popcorn and cranberries,
lighted candles in their holders and chains of red and green paper links
fashioned by children's hands in preparation for the glorious feast.

The room is transformed as the years drop away.
The rain is suddenly silent as if drowned out
By the cheerful singing voices of the happy expectant family
For the visit of the Christ child.

I move into the stilled bedroom where as a child I had lain
in my solitary sleeplessness. Waiting in tears for the family to retire
or to rescue me from the imagined terrors of the dark room
and the peering window that overlooked my couch. The kitchen that
had once been the center of family gathers cluttered now with debris.
The windows obscured with dust, cobwebs and the curtain of rain
dripping from the eaves outside. The stove that once had exuded
warmth and tantalizing odors—
no longer there. A vacant spot where once the happy table stood.

Looking through the back door the yard that had once been cleared
by the vigorous action of children and pets
now overgrown and filled with weeds
and memories of children's games.

POW: Promises Kept

The only color in a grown up hedgerow overshadowed
by dripping mulberries—
a wild rose peering out of the foliage
signifying the spirit of joy
that had once inhabited this small plot.

Battles once won—once lost
appear before me for a fleeting instant
then vanish in a clap of thunder
and a sudden downpour.

As I stepped from the front porch and dashed through the rain
I glanced back through the dusk for one more look.
The door, still ajar, and the darkened windows seemed to say,
"Come back. Come back to where your childhood took bloom,
and rekindle that diminishing spark
that has long lain waiting."

Upon an early, rainy Sunday visit to my childhood home,
now vacant and abandoned.

Beech Street house

BOOTS ON THE GROUND

RENDEZVOUS WITH DESTINY

President Roosevelt began the first peacetime draft in 1940, requiring the registration of all men between the ages of 21 to 45. However, after the attack on Pearl Harbor, the age range was amended dropping it from 21 years to 18.

Boots received his notice at the age of 19. He answered because he believed the same as FDR, who said, "There is a mysterious cycle in human events. To some generations much is given. Of other generations much is expected. This generation of Americans has a rendezvous with destiny."

He was sent to Camp Robinson in North Little Rock, Arkansas, with the other volunteers to get their physicals. Half of the young men were turned down because of malnutrition, a result of the Great Depression.

The ones who passed the physicals took the army classification test. Those who scored low were sent to the ground forces, which meant the Infantry. Those who scored high were eligible for the Air Corps. Boots scored high. It just so happened that while he was at Camp Robinson a notice was put out that the government needed young men between the ages of 18 and 21 who had scored high on the classification test to join the Army Air Corps. Since childhood, Boots had been fascinated with aviation. He volunteered.

While Boots spoke about his experience at Camp Robinson, he paused, reflected a moment and said, "I feel my generation was prepared for hard times due to the depression."

Indeed, this generation knew how to survive with little complaint.

He was sent to the Amarillo Army Airfield in Texas for ten weeks of basic training. There he undertook a rigorous schedule consisting of close order drills, long hikes, field maneuvers, qualifying on the rifle range and studying the Manual of Arms.

At that time the American military was ranked 17th in the world. Training was interesting, to say the least. The men trained in the fields with stovepipes to represent cannon and mortars. They drilled with brooms as rifles. Trucks had signs on them that read, *this is a tank.* During WWII a horse cavalry was still being used.

When Boots volunteered for the Air Corps he had visions of being a fighter pilot. He could see himself as an Ace wearing a long white scarf blowing in the wind. However, when the psychiatrist examined him, he said, "Boots, you don't have the killer instinct, you'll never make it." So Boots was sent to gunnery school in Kingman, Arizona to train as an aerial gunner.

After training he went to aircraft armor school in Denver to study turrets for 50 caliber machine guns. He left Denver and went to Sioux City, Iowa and there his team was put together. The crew consisted of pilot Joseph Ellis, co-pilot William Seat, navigator George Bartnik, engineer/gunner Walter Paskon, radio operator Mark Golsch, ball turret gunner Donald Carl, gunners Wayne Elkin, Boots Mayberry and Glenn Wright—who was the youngest on the crew, age seventeen. The pilot was the oldest at twenty-two. These men became like family to him. Their lives interlocked because they depended on one another for survival.

From Sioux City, the crew went to Lincoln Nebraska to await orders to go overseas. In November of 1944, the guys decided to see a movie,

Boots, before going overseas

Laura. While watching the show a directive flashed on the screen for all combat crews to report to the flight line. When they arrived they were assigned to a new B17 G aircraft and were bound to the European Theater of Operations.

Boots said he always wondered how the movie ended. Years later, he watched it again with his wife, Marion, and found himself watching for the order, *Report to flight line!*

The aircraft took off in a snowstorm and headed northeast. When they flew over Chicago, the navigator said, "All right, men. Look down and see the last of my hometown for a long time."

Their last stop was at Dow Field in Bangor, Maine, before leaving American soil. This great adventure for Boots had a bittersweet feel. He recalls staring out the waist-high window at the earth below and wondering, "Will I ever see America again?"

AWOL? ALREADY?

Boots's overseas adventure began with a bang once the crew landed in Holy Head, Wales. From there they were supposed to catch a train to Stone, England where they were attached to the 388th Bomb Group.

While waiting for the train, Boots and Mark Golsch, the radio operator, decided to visit a teashop close by. The waitress was a lovely girl and soon she had two yanks hanging on her every word. Boots and Mark were so engrossed with this young English lass that they missed their troop train.

AWOL on their first day!

Mark looked around the station, shoved his hands in his pockets, then asked in a worried voice, "Boots, what do you think we should do?"

Boots lifted his eyebrows and grinned. "I think we should go back in and have another cup of tea."

Before they returned to visit with the cute waitress they found the stationmaster and told him what had happened. He advised them to buy tickets to Stone, England and with a knowing look added, "The officers will be looking for you."

When they finally arrived in Stone that evening and joined their team, the pilot blew out a relieved sigh and said, "Whew, I didn't know if you were going to make it or not, Mayberry."

While Boots told this story, I had the feeling that if he had it to do all over again, he would still have had that cup of tea served by the lovely young waitress.

FIRST MISSION

The first of December, Boots and his crewmates arrived in England. They belonged to the 560th Squadron. The base was dispersed across the countryside. The Operations Area—bombs, planes, and runway—were in a separate location from where the crews lived. This was a safety precaution since the airfields had been attacked earlier in the war. Had the crews been kept close to Operations, they would have all perished.

The Quonset huts where they stayed were many miles from the mess halls and airplanes, so the soldiers bought bicycles for transportation. This helped them familiarize themselves with English countryside and acclimate to the weather. Soon after they arrived each member of the team went to separate training sessions, the pilots with pilots from other crews, gunners with other gunners.

Wintertime flying in England during the war was a dangerous venture. The airmen had state of the art oxygen that allowed each crewmember to be individually connected. They wore heated suits with a rheostat in order for them to control the temperature, which was important because in flight the temperature fell to sub-zero temperatures, 40 degrees to 60 degrees below. The crew didn't dare touch metal. When they spoke the moisture from their breath would freeze in the oxygen mask airway and they'd have to squeeze it to break the ice that had formed in the

B-17 Flying Fortress

tube so the oxygen would continue to flow making it possible for them to breathe. The suit they wore was always in danger of shorting out due to perspiration, which they certainly did during combat. If the suit quit working the airman had approximately seven to eight minutes to survive before freezing to death. And the mission would not be aborted for one man. They were considered expendable.

In late December they flew their first mission. They were to bomb Ludwigshafen, Germany. Boots describes this mission as a *disaster.* On the way to their target the oxygen system failed and the pilot had to drop below the bombing altitude in order for the crew to take off their masks and breathe. The flight commander issued an order for them to return to base. And so they did, with a full bomb load, five thousand pounds, and without a fighter escort. Boots's position was only eight feet away from the bomb bay, which made for a tense ride home. After that first mission, the team continued to work together and with each subsequent flight they became finely honed and worked as one man.

The number of missions required at that time was twenty-five. However, toward the end of the war, the number of missions required from each crew was raised from twenty-five to thirty . Five seems like a small number. But not in this case. The men had often wondered if they would survive through twenty-five missions much less thirty.

A SNOWBALL'S CHANCE

After five missions, Boots and his crew were given a three-day pass to London. Boots had never been to a city larger than Little Rock, Arkansas and now he found himself in one of the largest cities in the world. They visited a Red Cross facility named the Rainbow Red Cross in Piccadilly Circus. In the center of Piccadilly was a statue of Eros, the Greek god of love. Soldiers from all over—Belgium, New Zealand, Australia, England, and the United States—rested on the steps at the base of the statue or milled around the street. A Bobby, the British name for their policemen, strolled through the crowd to keep order.

While they loitered about, a heavy snow began to fall. Soon the ground was covered. From somewhere in the crowd, a snowball flew across the street and hit the Bobby on his helmet. Then another hit Boots's friend Wayne. No one to miss a good snowball fight, Boots scooped up a handful of snow, shaped it in a ball and threw it into the crowd. Soon, hundreds of snowballs zinged through the air. The Bobby blew his whistle, calling for help with this unruly crowd, but that only served to incite more snowballs. It was a snowball battle, congesting traffic, creating mayhem and frustrating the law. But in general, it was good, clean, fun.

Piccadilly, where the snowballs flew!

Boots looked at me after telling me this story, smiled and said, "Why can't they settle wars like this? Put leaders in a large place and let them fight it out? "

It was times like these that were invaluable in keeping up a soldier's spirit. Opportunities to do this were scarce but, when they came, the soldiers took full advantage of them.

PAYING WINSTON A VISIT

Later, Boots and his crew went back to London on another three-day leave. They hadn't been there two hours before a couple of his crewmembers were picked up and taken to jail by the Military Police for disorderly conduct in a Pub.

The men were held for a few hours to sober up and then released because combat soldiers wouldn't be kept incarcerated. When they were freed, they set out and found Boots. By now, all the fellows were feeling pretty good due to the pub offerings and they discussed what they should do with the rest of their evening. One said, "We're close to #10 Downing Street. Let's go call on Winston Churchill. Tell him the Yanks are here and for him to not worry about a thing."

Well, that sounded like an excellent idea so they stumbled toward the Churchill abode. At the time, Downing was a small neighborhood. Number 10 had a modest courtyard with no security at all. Boots and his buddies walked right up to the front door and began pounding.

A huge Bobby answered the door and looked down at the ragtag bunch of inebriated Yanks and said, "May I help you?"

"Yes," answered one of the friends. "We want to see Winston. Tell him we're here."

"I have two things to say to you," said the imposing fellow. "First, Mr. Churchill is not here. Secondly, I suggest you get your blooming arses back to your squadron before I make you sorry you came here in the first place."

Boots knew right away this Bobby who towered over them meant business and so he gave a little wave and said before he left, "Well, tell Winston we called."

You know, I can't help but think that if Mr. Churchill had answered the door, he would have invited Boots and the boys in and had a drink with them. Poor Winston. He never had the pleasure of meeting Boots Mayberry.

CHOIRBOY

On Christmas Eve, 1944, Boots felt homesick. He missed his family on this special holiday and wanted to attend a midnight mass. The base didn't have a chapel so he decided to walk to the little village of Coney Weston where he attended the Church of England called St. Mary's. This lovely little church was four hundred years old. Coal stoves warmed the building and its only source of light were candles.

He asked if anyone wanted to go with him, but no one did, so he struck out alone. He walked two miles in the winter wonderland. Each step crunched on the snow-covered ground. When he came to the church it was as if he'd walked back in time. The fir trees and church roof were bedecked with glistening white. The windows glowed with flickering candlelight that reflected on the snow drifts in the yard. The scene made him think of a Dickens novel.

The church was full of GI's, all in full uniform. He felt underdressed but went inside anyway. In one of the rows he noticed an empty spot with a music folio on the seat. He pushed his way between the men, picked up the folio and sat, wondering why the men kept giving him strange looks.

After some readings from the Old and New Testament, the announcement was made that the choir was going to sing *Silent Night.*

Where Boots became a choirboy

The guys around him picked up their music and stood. It was then Boots realized he'd insinuated himself in the choir. There was nothing left to do but grab his music, stand, and sing his best. And that he did. He must have impressed the organist, ninety-year-old Alice Bloomfield, because she sent him Christmas cards for several years after he returned home.

A new year was upon him. In less than two months he'd fly a mission to Germany. It would be his last time to see England.

THE LAST MISSION

On February 20, 1945, Boots and his crew were assigned to fly to Nuremberg, Germany, hit their target, a munitions factory, and fly home. They were also supposed to drop chaff, which was like a bundle of metallic Christmas tree tinsel designed to throw off the radar of the ground guns firing at the planes. A routine flight, one like the many they had done before.

The day dawned with miserable weather, cold and wet. And if that wasn't bad enough, they also were in the worst possible position a plane could be, the tail end, sometimes called *Tail End Charley* or *Purple Heart Corner*. However, after take-off the weather cleared up and they had a good visual of the ground. But having a good visual of the ground was a double-edged sword because those on the ground could see them as well.

The flight was uneventful. They didn't encounter any fighters. Boots and the men looked forward to dropping their load and going home. They approached Nuremberg, lined up with their target and the bomb doors were opened. Suddenly from the ground a box barrage of anti-aircraft fire was sent up. A huge black cloud of metallic splinters burst under the plane and caused it to rock. Holes were blown through the aluminum fuselage. Boots called them *Little Black Flowers that bloomed in the sky*. Two bursts hit close. The third hit the right wing on the in-board engine and it caught fire. This was only eight feet from the five-thousand-pound bomb load. Even in that deadly situation the pilot didn't give orders to bail out. He told his men, "We didn't come all this distance not to do what we came to do." So, with the plane on fire, they delivered the load and hit the target.

The minute the bombs were dropped the pilot attempted to put the fire out by diving the plane. He put it into a dive from twenty-five thousand feet down to thirteen thousand feet before pulling out. The centrifugal force pushed the crew to the floor. At first it appeared that the fire had gone out, but it reignited. There was nothing left to do for the pilot but to give the order for everyone to bail out, then he put the plane on autopilot.

Everything was in anxious confusion. Boots kicked open his hatch and a wall of black smoke and flame covered the opening. Glenn Wright, the seventeen-year-old tail gunner, climbed up from the turret yelling over the din that he couldn't get his hatch open. Boots told him to go ahead of him and jump. But when Glenn kneeled down at the opening and saw the smoke and flames, he froze. Boots felt at any second the plane might blow, so he put his boot between the boy's shoulder blades, pushed him out and then jumped out behind him. He wasn't real confident about how to use the parachute—he never thought he'd need to—but he remembered being told to pull the red handle.

While telling me this, he stopped, chuckled a bit and said, "When we were issued the parachutes at our base, the supply sergeant had a dark sense of humor. He said to us, 'If it doesn't work, return it and I'll give you another.' Thank goodness mine worked."

When Boots bailed out, he couldn't tell where he was in relation to the ground and didn't realize he was falling head first with his feet up. When he pulled the ripcord it jerked him around with such force two vertebrae in his neck broke. He didn't realize this at the time, but he knew something was wrong because he had lost the use of his hands and couldn't guide his parachute. As a result, he floated aimlessly to earth under a thirty-foot silk canopy.

All around him was a cacophony of anti-aircraft fire. Shrapnel and wreckage from destroyed airplanes hurtled past him. Fear and dread filled his mind. *What if this wreckage hit him or his parachute and dragged him down to certain death?* In the deafening noise of all this melee, he cried out, "God, help me."

In the distance he saw an American fighter plane, a P51 Mustang, flying toward him. The soldiers called them *Little Friends*. The pilot saw Boots's predicament and began circling around Boots to protect him as best he could at great personal risk to himself. The pilot continued to circle as long as he possibly could and still have enough fuel to make it back to the base. On the last pass, he flew close to Boots. So close, Boots could see the pilot's eyes above his oxygen mask. Then the pilot saluted.

Boots stopped speaking at this point in the story, looked down at the table and drummed his fingers a few seconds. Then he looked at me and said, "In the military you either salute Hello or Goodbye. The pilot probably thought this was *Goodbye* for me. He honored me with a final salute. Then when he left for home base he did a victory roll away."

While Boots told me about this, I could see that even after all these years that pilot's act of respect and compassion still deeply touched Boots. Even though it seemed like a hopeless situation, the pilot still did what he could for Boots.

When I left Boots's home that afternoon, I thought about that pilot and how he did what he could no matter how hopeless the situation seemed, No matter how small, acts of respect and kindness are powerful things.

Since that day, I've watched for opportunities to follow that pilot's example.

Greater love has no one than this,
that one lay down his life for his friends.
                                        ~John 15:13

A "Little Friend" or a guardian angel?

PRISONER OF WAR

Boots saw people gathering below as he drifted toward a large open field that had been prepared for spring plowing. The locals didn't like or trust the American airmen. They called them *Air Gangsters*. Thankfully German soldiers rescued him from the angry farmers and took him to jail. There the German police searched him and confiscated his escape kit which held maps, compasses, and survival things.

Boots was held for ten days in solitary at a German aerodrome. He received no medical attention at all. While there he wondered what had happened to his crew. Sleet and snow added to Boots's agony. The frigid weather compounded the pain from his injuries. On the eleventh day they put him on a wood burning bus that was run by steam. . On the bus he saw one of his crewmembers, a fellow who normally didn't fly missions with them, but happened to be on the fated flight because he was checking special radar equipment.

Boots noticed another thing on that bus—his parachute and all his gear. He focused on the yellow ribbon his girlfriend had given him. Most airmen took a memento that held a special meaning with them into battle. She had drawn a sun, moon, and stars on it and he had tied it to his harness. In that miserable cold, in his pain and despair, that ribbon was like a shining star. An odd thing to note, the day Boot's plane was shot down was his girlfriend's birthday. While he stared at that ribbon, he felt he had passed from being a young man to becoming an old man. He knew he would never be the same after the war. That is, if he survived.

The guards fed him once a day, the same thing every day—headcheese—a meat aspic that contained the trimmings from pork or bovine sculls as well as pieces of internal organs. He didn't like it at all, but ate it anyway.

Air raids blared every night. In the pitch blackness he could hear the shuffle of the guards' boots as they scurried to the bomb shelters, leaving the prisoners in harm's way. But this proved to be a good thing. In all the noise and with the guards being gone he learned there were two other Americans, both officers, also waiting to be taken to interrogation. While the guards were in the shelters, the prisoners shouted back and forth. It felt good to know that comrades were near.

The day came when Boots and the other prisoners were taken to Frankfort and held in a Dulag Luft, which was the name given to Prisoner of War transit camps for Air Corps captives. The soldiers called the camp a *sweatbox* because the interrogators would try to *sweat* the information out of them. They kept him there a week, interrogating him daily. The Germans who questioned him spoke perfect English and used any kind of psychological and physical means to get information. Boots told only his name, rank, and serial number. After they were finished with him in Frankfort he was taken to Stalag Luft #13 in Nuremberg.

At this point, the German commanders knew they had lost the war. Their country was in complete shambles. Their cities were in rubble and their citizens wandered the streets looking for food and family members. America demanded an unconditional surrender, but the Germans hoped for better peace terms so they used the prisoners as pawns for bargaining power.

When the American Army came too close to a prison camp the prisoners were made to move, no matter if they were injured, sick or malnourished. If they could walk, they had to go. Sometimes they were forced to walk for miles. The German guards were mostly older men who could no longer fight on the front and had been assigned to prison camps. Just like the prisoners, they were weak from hunger. It wasn't unusual for the stronger Americans to volunteer and help the older guards by carrying their rifles and backpacks for them. Other times the prisoners were transported in cattle cars, jammed so tight inside that they had to take turns sitting and standing.

The stock cars did not have any markings to indicate prisoners of war were onboard, so U.S. Army fighters often fired on them. That happened once when Boots was being transported. The engine had been shot and disabled, so the guards let the prisoners out. Thankfully, when the fighter pilots saw the prisoners standing by the train, they flew off realizing there were American and allied P.O.W.s being transported.

Steam and hot water spewed from the train's engine. Not ones to miss such a great opportunity, the English soldiers took the small tin cups they carried with them, and pulled the old, often-used teabags from their pockets, then proceeded to catch the hot water in their cups.

It was highly doubtful that these bags produced even a hint of tea, but perhaps this bit of home brought comfort.

What no mother ever wants to see

THE REAL HEROES

Many times while Boots told me his experiences during the war, he would interject, rather emphatically at times, "Don't make me out a hero. I wasn't. I was just doing what I took an oath to do. The real heroes were the ones waiting back home. They didn't know where we were, or if we were hurt or alive. But they kept the faith. They waited and prayed."

I can't imagine what Boots's mother felt when she received the telegram informing her that her son went missing in action. My throat constricts every time I read the telegram even though I know Boots made it home safe and sound.

Boots continued on about his mother—his hero, "My mother had two sons in the war. She did all she could to support the war effort. She purchased war bonds and stamps, belonged to a group called *The Army Mothers' Club*, and served many hours feeding local based and visiting service men and women. Mother was a strong character and strong in her Christian faith. She prayed and believed that her boys would return from the war safe and intact. God bless her."

Amen to that. And God bless the heroes who wait at home today.

What they fought against

PROMISES

Although Boots had attended church and heard the pastor tell about God and his son, Jesus, he never really paid attention. He never gave much thought about how God loved him and cared about his welfare. However, while drifting over that plowed field with debris hurdling past and ammo firing around him, he cried out from the center of his being, "God help me."

God heard.

While in Stalag Luft #13 in Nuremberg, Boots became deathly ill. One night his friend Wayne Elkin noticed Boot's violent shivering from fever and the damp, frigid weather. He took off his overcoat and covered Boots to warm him. The next morning Boots was too sick and weak to make roll call so he was moved to a building where those who were dying or had already died were kept to get them out of the way.

After spending several days in the dank gloom of that room, a guard walked in and announced the American and Allied forces were advancing close to camp and they were going to have to evacuate and go to another camp. He said, "All of you who can fall out, do so. The rest of you will be left behind."

Boots didn't want to be left behind, alone. So he got to his hands and knees and crawled toward the door. He noticed something lying on the floor and inched toward it. In the dim, dusky, light he found a pocket-sized New Testament and Psalms, perhaps belonging to another prisoner who'd either died or dropped it in despair. The tiny Bible was opened to Psalm 91. He bent closer and read:

Whoever dwells in the shelter of the Most High will rest in the shadow of the Almighty.

I will say of the Lord, "He is my refuge and my fortress, my God, in whom I trust."

Surely he will save you from the fowler's snare and from the deadly pestilence.

He will cover you with his feathers, and under his wings you will find refuge; his faithfulness will be your shield and rampart.

You will not fear the terror of night, nor the arrow that flies by day, nor the pestilence that stalks in the darkness, nor the plague that destroys at midday.

A thousand may fall at your side, ten thousand at your right hand, but it will not come near you.

You will only observe with your eyes and see the punishment of the wicked.

If you say, "The Lord is my refuge," and you make the Most High your dwelling, no harm will overtake you, no disaster will come near your tent.

For he will command his angels concerning you to guard you in all your ways; they will lift you up in their hands, so that you will not strike your foot against a stone.

You will tread on the lion and the cobra; you will trample the great lion and the serpent.

"Because he loves me," says the Lord, "I will rescue him; I will protect him, for he acknowledges my name.

He will call on me, and I will answer him; I will be with him in trouble, I will deliver him and honor him.

With long life I will satisfy him and show him my salvation."
– NIV (emphasis added)

There is a saying that *you know that you know that you know.* Boots knew that in that dark room of death, he'd heard from God. He picked up the Testament, put it in his shirt pocket, crawled out the door and made the journey to the next camp, Stalag 7A, Moosburg, Germany.

Found in the POW camp . . .

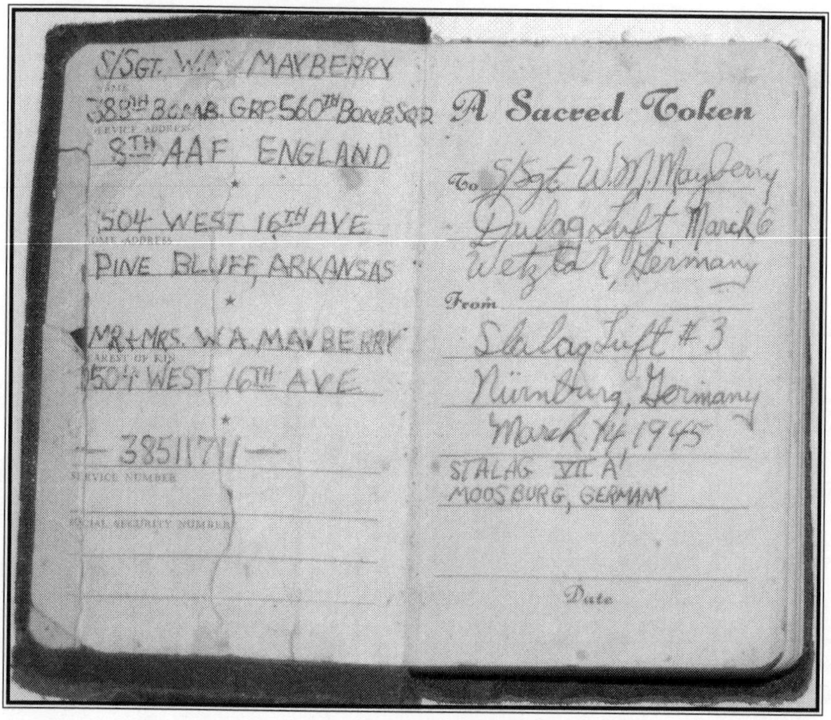

. . . his salvation

MORE PROMISES

The prisoners had to walk to Stalag 7A in Moosburg, which was seven miles from the Dachau extermination camp. The air was filled with the stench of smoke pumped out of the cremation chimneys.

In Moosburg 7A there were thousands of prisoners, both American and Allied. Some had been in the camp for five years. The only shelters were dilapidated barracks left over from WWI or flimsy tents that did little to shelter against the cold. Even though it was April, the snow and sleet still fell and the freezing wind bit their skin.

When the older prisoners saw Boots's condition, they took him under their care, shared what little food they had, and nursed him back to health. Prisoners scoured the fields and trash searching for anything edible. They found rotten carrots, beets, turnip tops and such. Some of the soldiers had been able to procure powdered milk and powdered coffee in Red Cross parcels. The English soldiers had made tiny cook stoves out of tin cans and called them *blowers*, which operated on the order of blacksmith's billows. Inside the cans they had fashioned little fans that when turned could make hot fires with just a few twigs. On top was a small place to put a cup in order to heat water. Every night the men enjoyed a cup of hot coffee.

The prisoners were assigned jobs and Boots's assignment was to work on the railroad and rebuild what had been bombed. While on the outside of the camp he had access to junk and trash so he scrounged around and found wire, pipe, and such to use for building radios and tools. His friend Wayne fashioned spoons for them out of some of the wire and tin. Boots still has his and it is a prized possession.

Before being taken prisoner in Germany, Boots didn't make fast friends with anyone but his crew. This was common among the soldiers. They avoided making friends with those outside of their team because more than likely they wouldn't come back. New soldiers would try to show pictures of their children or sweethearts but the older soldiers would hold up their hands and say, "No, I don't want to see any pictures." It was a protection to know as little about each other as possible. However, as prisoners, that all changed. During the evenings the prisoners sat around and talked about their hometown to keep from thinking about how hungry they were. Their conversation centered on two things: food and going home.

When the talk turned to the possibility of not making it home, they asked for and made promises to each other. The conversation went something like this, "I've always wanted to have a big family. If I don't make it would you have one for me?" "I want a college education. If I don't get back, would you go to college for me?" "I want to have a meaningful job." "I've always wanted to play golf." "I've always wanted to write a book."

They would all agree and say, "If you don't get back, we will try to do that for you."

One soldier shared that he had lived his whole life where the water supply was limited so he used to take baths in the gutter after it had rained. He recalled how he loved splashing about. He said that when he got home, after a gully-washer, he wanted to take his shoes off and wade in the gutter. And if he didn't get back? Boots promised he'd do it for him.

Years later, Boots learned this soldier never made it home. So when it rained and the street gutters were full, he kicked off his shoes and waded in, splashing to beat the band. Cars drove by sending sprays of water over him, probably wondering why that old gray-haired man was playing in the rain.

Boots had a great time keeping this promise. It was as if that soldier from long ago had given Boots a gift.

After he'd shared that memory with me he recited the last verse of Robert Frost's poem, *Stopping by the Woods on a Snowy Evening* because it eloquently expresses the dedication he has toward the promises he made to those men, his comrades, in that prison camp;

The woods are lovely, dark and deep,
But I have promises to keep,
And miles to go before I sleep,
And miles to go before I sleep.

Boots has been faithful to try to keep the promises he made. He has a wonderful family. At the age of eighty-one he received his associate's degree. He worked twenty-five years as an air traffic controller. He shoots a good round of golf and has published a book of poetry titled, A Distant Drummer.

LIBERATION!

On April 12, 1945 an announcement to the Americans was made over the internment camp speaker. "Your president, Franklin Roosevelt, is dead. Your great leader is no longer with you." Of course, no one believed it. This was nothing new. Their captors were always trying to lower the prisoners' already-low morale. But while the men didn't believe what they thought was propaganda, they did have a feeling that something was about to happen. Boots could hear tank diesel engines running as the Germans retreated, abandoning Moosburg, signaling that the United States Army was approaching and the camp would fall.

On the Saturday night before liberation the next day, what Boots calls Liberation Sunday, it was sleeting. He walked to the outer edge of camp and saw a young German soldier around his age patrolling the camp. Boots had learned just enough German to communicate on a very basic level. The German soldier knew just enough English. So they struck up a conversation. Boots asked, "All is kaput?" To which the young man guarding the camp answered, "Yes."

After a few minutes speaking along those lines Boots made a radical suggestion. He asked the soldier to surrender in order to save his life. Boots knew the remaining German soldiers would not give up without fight. If this young fellow were a POW, he would be protected and cared for. But the soldier refused.

Sunday morning the sun rose, a brilliant light in a clear blue sky. The red Nazi flag with a black swastika blazoned above black and white laurel leaves, brandished over the camp as it had for years. In the distance the approach of the American army rumbled. Just as Boots thought, the remaining Germans didn't surrender. A three-hour battle ensued before the United States Army prevailed.

After the combat, the American prisoners watched with pride as the Swastika slid down the pole and the Stars and Stripes rose to the top and waved gloriously over their heads.

Later the sad business of collecting the dead had to be done before leaving. The soldiers gathered the corpses of the German soldiers and laid them together. Boots walked by and saw the body of the young man he'd tried to talk into surrendering.

From Moosburg, the freed men were taken to France where they received much-needed medical attention. It was there that an army physician asked Boots how he'd broken his neck. Boots looked at the doctor and said, "I never knew I had." Then he remembered back when his plane was shot down and how, after he'd bailed out, the parachute snapped him around when he pulled the ripcord. He realized then why he had not been able to use his hands. When he told the doctor he'd never received any medical attention, the physician shook his head and said, "It is a miracle you can use your hands at all."

It was indeed a miracle. One of many.

GOING HOME

In France, at a Recovered Allied Military Personnel camp, Boots got a new uniform and then went to Le Havre to catch the SS William T Barry, a liberty ship, to go home. They sailed in a huge convoy patrolled by Canadian destroyers and US ships because there were German submarines that hadn't given up. It took three weeks to arrive at the United States.

The end of the war was a confusing time in England. The officials struggled to find information in order to send notices about whether prisoners were alive or dead. When Boots's ship docked in New Jersey, the first thing he did was to call his mother, collect. The operator in Pine Bluff knew the family and knew at that time the Mayberry's had two sons, both Staff Sergeants. Since the beginning of the war she had the sad duty of connecting families with bad news and the joyful duty of connecting them with good news. She couldn't help but to be emotionally involved. Imagine how she must have felt when she rang up Boots's mother. He listened as the operator said, "I have a collect call from Staff Sergeant Mayberry."

There was a pause and then his mother asked, "Which one?"

The operator answered, "It's Walter."

A long silence followed. No one could talk. Not Boots, his mother, or even the operator. This was the first inkling his mother had that Boots was alive. When Boots and his mother found their voices, they had a short conversation with the promise of a good long talk when he got home.

His mother had kept the faith, served her country, and her prayers had been answered. Both her boys were alive and intact.

He arrived in Pine Bluff two weeks later to a hero's welcome. For his twenty-eight months of service he received the following medals: The Purple Heart, Air Medal, P.O.W Medal, Presidential Unit Award, WWII Victory Medal, Good Conduct Medal, The Legion of Honor Medal (France's highest honor) and several campaign ribbons. He was honorably discharged on November 21, 1945.

However, as far as he was concerned, he was returning to the real heroes, his mother and family.

It's over!

ALWAYS BELIEVE IN DREAMS

Boots's First Attempt at Poetry

Oh I never believed in dreams,
never knew that they came true
till the night I dreamed of Heaven
and met an angel like you.

No, I never knew dreams were real,
never knew what they could start
till the day that I first met you
and let a dream walk off with my heart.

From the moment I saw you smile
I knew you were meant for my arms.
for how could I ever resist
the magic of your charms?

Your eyes are as bright as the stars,
that shine up in the blue,
and when I look at them
all my dreams, I know, are true.

So now I'll always believe in dreams,
never doubt what they can do.
And I'll go on dreaming darling,
till I'm with an angel that's you.

"The above lines were composed and scratched with a pin on the wall of a cell in a jail in Ansbach, Germany, four days after being shot down over Nuremberg, Germany, while on a bombing mission. Captured and taken to this jail where eleven days were spent in a solitary cell. It was in this way that I passed aerodrome time. This is the only composition that I remember. Perhaps it is better that it is."

RETURN TO KNETTISHALL

by Boots Mayberry

Tonight, on the edge of this small English village,
I stand—looking over familiar scenes that flood my mind
with memories of things long past.

Before me, now distorted shapes in the gathering darkness,
stands a row of barracks, quiet and deserted.
Shelters that once knew the voices of many men, walls that knew
their dark
and lonely hours, and shared their happiness and their sorrows,
that once listened to tales of home or war. Once-friendly places
now empty, deathly still and stark in the misty night.

Underfoot I tread the paths that felt the step of a G.I. shoe and heavy
flying boot. Paths that seem to sense the feeling of footsteps known
long ago,
now overgrown and reclaimed by the creeping grass.

Before me I see long ribbons of white stretching off through fields of
English countryside.

Seemingly endless strips that once felt the weight of a
thousand warplanes,
heavily laden with men and death for those who waited below.
Strips now deserted and like the paths, slowly being reclaimed by the
foraging weeds.

The quiet now presses in on me in violent waves,
as if it would suddenly burst forth in an eruption of all the familiar
sounds I knew.
There, suddenly, in front of me out of the darkness
I hear the noise of a hundred giant engines thundering in the morning air.
I hear the quiet voices of men talking, soon to go off into the dawn
in the gigantic metal birds.
Out on the strip I see a thousand khaki-clad warriors in endless rows,
marching to the heart-stirring strains of martial music,
their guidons and colors whipping in the breeze.

As I stand there transfixed, all of it is gone as suddenly as it appeared,
and I am alone again with the quiet and darkness.
I breathe a lonely sigh, for all these things are gone, never to return,
only to live in dark recesses of the mind brought forth again
in moments of wakefulness.
As I turn for a last look at the darkened spot I see again,
for a fleeting instant, those silver giants taking to the air for the last time
in the darkness of dawn.
I hear the vibrant sound of their roaring engines straining to raise
them airborne.
I hear the low murmur of voices saying last-minute good lucks,
and the thunderous roll call of men long gone before.
I hear music and the sound of their marching feet mingled with the
engines' roar

echoing down the dark corridors of time.
As their shapes disappear into the dusk of years
I feel a great sorrow, the sting of tears, and lift a heavy hand
in a final salute.

BOOTSY BOY

By Boots Mayberry

Oh! Bootsy Boy I left you behind
this day fifty years ago.
I left behind the little boy
Of cowboys, blocks and trikes.
Of Sixth Avenue and First Christian
of Vacation Bible School
and ball games at Oakland Park.
Bicycles and paper routes
band practice and football parades
Saturday matinees and
peanut butter kisses.

I left behind the short-in-the-top
and high-in-the-back haircuts.
The evening meals with the family
in the warmth of a winter's night.
The Friday night date to the movies
and the walk to the Snak Shop afterwards.
Hand-in-hand with the girl next door
in crinoline and auburn braids.

POW: Promises Kept

I left behind the football dances
at the Airport Club—the lights down low.
A lovely melody, holding her close,
the touch of her cheek, the fragrance
of her hair, the softness of her kiss.

I left behind the sunrise on the glint
of wild wings and the chug
of the top water bait awaiting the
strike of the black bass in the cool
of early morn.

I left behind walking the girls
homeward after school, pushing
our bikes along their side
as they clasped books to their breasts.
Pleated shirts and sweaters
buttoned up the back, white bobby socks
and dirty saddles. Smiling eyes and
pearly teeth behind bright lipstick.
The walk was too short.
Now it is time for a letter.
"Your friends and neighbors send you greeting.
Report for induction.
Army of the United States.

I leave you behind, young boy.
I meet you face-to-face young man.
I step out with you into the newness of life
never to look back for it only brings
the tear and the distant music and
laughter of yesterday.

Bootsy boy

SERVICE PICTURES

You're in the Army now!

Boots enters the Air Corps

Aircrewman Boots

All the crew

BOOTS MARCHING ONWARD

Boots, Marion, and daughters.

HOME

The old saying, *you can never go home*, was true for most World War II vets. While nothing may have changed in their towns, their houses, or in their families, the men themselves had changed. The shadows of war haunted Boots. He tried to silence them with alcohol and isolated himself to be in his own misery. Friendship was out of the question as a result from the days in service when he flew missions in Germany. A lot of men were lost in battle and new ones arrived to replace them. No one wanted to know anything about the new arrivals' families or lives. These men knew all too well the pain of getting attached then learning that their friends would never return from their missions, leaving a barrack full of empty bunks. Memories of lost comrades and being shut up in a prison made Boots feel as if he were locked in a shell.

While trying to decide what he wanted to do with the rest of his life, he thought about becoming a journalist. He applied for the GI Bill and enrolled in a summer course at the Arkansas State Teacher's College in Conway, AR. A decision he now says was made too soon after the war. Emotionally and mentally, he just wasn't ready. His professor assigned the class to write about what they had been doing the past three years. Boots wrote about his experiences in the war and being held in a prison camp, then turned it in. The following day the professor commented on each paper. When he got to Boots he said, "Well, if a person has something to say, he will find a way to say it no matter how *poorly* he does it."

That was a slap in Boots's face. Instead of encouraging him, the teacher humiliated him in front of everyone. Boots took the paper, tore it up and scattered it on the teacher's desk. Then he turned and walked out of the room. He never returned to that class.

Years later, Boots got an invitation to speak in Conway at a Fourth of July celebration in the Town Square. It was a festive, patriotic affair with flags and red, white, and blue balloons dancing in the breeze. There was also a Color Guard and a huge crowd waiting to give Boots a hero's welcome, which made him a little uncomfortable. He had a hard time visualizing himself as a hero. He considered himself a GI who did what he was called to do.

He began with this opening remark, "Years ago, I was a student in this town at Arkansas State Teacher's College. I took a journalism class and wrote a thesis. The professor said, 'If you have something to say, you will find a way to say it even though it is poorly done.' All of you are going to have to listen to what I have to say, no matter how poorly it is done."

A ripple of good-natured laughter followed Boots's self-deprecating joke. After he finished his speech, a man came to shake his hand. It was the professor who had humiliated him. He said, "Boots, I want to apologize to you. Instead of encouraging you, I discouraged you from doing what you wanted to do. I want you to know that I have no doubt that you will find a way to help relieve those who are shut up in darkness."

The professor's prophecy would prove to be true in a big way later in Boots's life.

After his very short stint in college, Boots got a job working as a freight handler at the railroad. He was the smallest worker pushing a two-wheeled dolly. He worked twelve to fifteen hours a day, which suited him. He was too busy to think or feel. His health improved dramatically from all the heavy lifting, pushing, and walking. He left that job to work for the Western Electric Company installing switchboards. This job change would also be the catalyst to a dramatic life change. A change that would bring him back home.

Working for the Cotton Belt

MARION

God's Gift

While he changed switchboards over to a dial system in Pine Bluff, Arkansas at the main office of the telephone company, a pretty little curly-headed operator caught his eye. Not only was she pretty, she had a charming personality. He asked one of the other operators about her and found her name was Marion Carruthers.

The chief operator didn't want her girls fraternizing with the Western Electric Men, so Boots had to find a sneaky way to get her attention. When he started working on the opposite side of Marion's board, he tossed her a note. She read it and tossed him one. Soon the notes were flying back and forth. Later they were formally introduced at a picnic and began dating.

Marion was a lot like Boots in that she was also a loner. At a tender age she experienced the pain of being left behind and unsettling change. When she was two, her mother contracted tuberculosis and suffered other illnesses as well. Her mother never left the hospital. Her father was left alone to raise eight children. The decision was made to put Marion and her two sisters in an Anglican orphanage in Memphis called The Sisters of St. Ann. She stayed there until she was ten, when she moved in with her grandmother in Collierville, Tennessee. Her father eventually remarried and brought her back to live with him and her new stepmother in Pine Bluff.

Boots and Marion dated for two years. He found her to be a classy lady who could talk about anything. He admired her strong character. And because they were both loners, they understood each other and meshed easily. Life was good. Boots enjoyed being a bachelor and dating the most beautiful young lady in town. Even so, he was reluctant to marry because he didn't want any responsibilities or to be vulnerable. He couldn't bring himself to risk commitment and then losing the one he loved.

On the other hand, Marion wanted to marry. One day she threw down the gauntlet. She told Boots if nothing was going to come of their relationship, she was going to leave Pine Bluff and move to Louisiana and live with her grandmother. Boots certainly didn't want to lose Marion so he borrowed five dollars from her, purchased a marriage license and ended his 26-year bachelorhood.

They married at the Pine Bluff Trinity Episcopal Church in 1949. He was on time but Marion was fifteen minutes late because her father worked on a barge and had to clean up. Boots remembers being so nervous that when it came time to say the vows his friend had to help him say the words.

As the years went by, Boots realized what a gift his Heavenly Father had given him in Marion. It was like going from a black and white life to a Technicolor one. She was his new beginning. The bad memories faded. He admired how she faced life squarely without fear or hesitation. She had a vision and followed it. And because of her, he found his vision too. Boots said of her, "Through the years I learned to love by her example. "

Marion went home to be with the Lord in March of 2012. She and Boots had been married sixty-two years and been blessed with three daughters: Jill, Robin and Edith, also known as Edie.

To describe the power of Marion's love in his life, Boots used a lyric from the song, *Love is a many Splendored Thing* and said, "Her fingers touched my silent heart and caused it to sing."

Flirting at the phone company

Boots & Marion, dating

Mr. & Mrs. Boots Mayberry!

FINALLY FREE

Even though Boots had been out of the service for years and walked the streets of Pine Bluff as a free man, he was still held in a mental and emotional prison. The bars that held him were hate, bitterness, and unforgiveness. Flashbacks of things that had happened to the people he'd known fed the animosity that tortured his soul. He had trouble sleeping because nightmares of war kept him awake.

One evening Boots and Marion visited a chapel appropriately named the Chapel of the Resurrection at Moore Community near Eureka Springs Arkansas. The priest read a lesson about the men who took their friend to Jesus for healing but couldn't get through the crowd. No willing to give up, they climbed on the roof, made an opening and lowered the man in front of Jesus. While listening to the sermon, the Lord gently asked, "Why are you still letting people who are no longer alive hurt you? Even though you were freed from the POW camp, you are still imprisoned by thoughts of unforgiveness."

Then the Lord brought to Boots's mind his first grandchild, Kelly. During the Vietnam War years his daughter, Jill, and her husband, Gary, were based at the very same hamlet in Germany where Boots had been captured thirty years before. Kelly was born in the hospital in Nuremberg, adjacent to the camp where he was held prisoner. The Lord assured him this was no coincidence. His little *joy gift* was born where his imprisonment began.

At that moment, Christ's love and light dawned in Boots's soul. He gave up the hate and bitterness and chose to forgive. Just like in prison camp when the German flag slid down the pole in defeat and the American flag was raised in victory, the flag of hate was defeated and love waved victoriously over Boots's soul and spirit. He was finally free.

BACK TO PRISON

It is wonderful what liberation does for a soul. Boots had been reconciled to his former enemies. He now recognized how his experience as a prisoner of war had made a pivotal change in his way of thinking and as a Christian. In fact, after Boots had given up his hate and bitterness, he began doing things he'd never done before.

He no longer sat in chapel as a pew warmer. Instead he became involved with his church and the community. Boots began a food pantry to feed the hungry and gathered clothing for the poor. He visited the sick in hospitals and in their homes. Together, he and Marion joined an ecumenical prayer group. They grew in their love for each other and their love for the Lord.

Little did Boots know that his liberation would send him back to prison.

He and Marion were members of an Episcopal church and had the opportunity to fly to Denver and attend the Episcopal convention. While there, the bishop asked Marion and Boots to read the lessons. Marion had no problem reading from the Old Testament. However, as Boots read from the New Testament, Marion had to hold on to him to keep him from shaking. Later, Boots decided to sit a while in the sun and relax a little. He noticed a television crew setting up around the pool. Thinking that some of the conference attendees may be interviewed, he mentally prepared himself for what he'd say about the church and the Spirit, just in case he were asked. Sure enough, a reporter tapped him on his shoulder and said, "Excuse me sir. May I ask you a few questions on what is going on in the Anglican Church? You don't have to say anything on your own. I'll ask the questions."

Boots said, "Sure."

When the cameras started rolling the reporter made her introduction then turned to Boots and asked, "What's your reflection on what is going on in the Anglican Church?"

The nerves that tormented Boots earlier were gone. Vanished. He started talking about how the Spirit was moving in the church and the reporter couldn't shut him up. Later he was told that the news spot wasn't just local, it was international. His friends from all over the country called him to say they'd seen him on television.

He'd caught another person's attention as well, the chairwoman of the Kairos Prison Ministry, an international organization just getting its start in Arkansas at that time. She'd heard he'd been a POW and approached him saying, "How would you like to go back to prison?"

Marion said, "We'd love to." But Boots said, "No way."

The next year the chairwoman called again with the same invitation. This time Marion had a *discussion* with Boots about becoming a part of this prison ministry and they came to the conclusion it was time to do it.

A group of forty people came together to train for Kairos. They met four consecutive Saturdays in order to pray and get to know each other as a team, which reminded Boots of the synergy he'd experienced in the military. The purpose of this ministry was to pray with the prisoners, share the love and forgiveness of Jesus Christ, teach a short introductory course on Christianity, share meals together and just talk with the prisoners on a one-to-one basis.

It all seemed easy enough. He and Marion were ready. They went to Tucker Prison near Pine Bluff. The guards opened the gate and he could see the chapel fifty yards away. The moment he stepped in he had a flashback to the tunnels in the German prison camp and how the camp surveyors made him to step off the number of yards to measure the distance between the fence and the nearest dwelling. Automatically he started counting paces to the chapel. Then he heard the gates slam shut. The sound shook him up so that he had to have the Chaplain help him regain his composure.

As time went on he grew more at ease. At first, when he stood to speak to the prisoners, they would yell, "Get out of here and leave us alone." They'd throw cups of water at him and run objects against the bars to serve notice of their disdain. But Boots knew he had a message to deliver and since they were a captive audience, they'd have to listen to him. When he started sharing with them stories about being a prisoner of war in Germany, they prisoners quieted. He had their complete and undivided attention. Standing before them was a man who understood about being locked down and put in hard labor. He was one of them. They connected with him as he gave the message that though they were imprisoned physically, they could be free spiritually.

Boots and Marion served together for eighteen years. Then Kairos began another outreach called Kairos Outside, a ministry to support the female loved ones of the men who were incarcerated. They moved to this branch of Kairos and served there in their later years.

Boots continues to impact the lives of others. He is still keeping promises he made to his fellow soldiers and God is still keeping His promise to give Boots a long life. Boots turned ninety-one on August 11, 2014.

His stories of hardship, bravery, and faith as recorded in this book are a gift to us all because of the wisdom and hope it brings. It is said that life is ten percent what happens to us and ninety percent with what we do with it. My hope is that all who read this book would endeavor to follow Boots's example and let go of the past, serve others in the present, and trust God for the future.

Kairos crosses

PAPA'S PRAYER

By Boots Mayberry

After the last little one has crept off to bed,
After the drop of each curl,
After I stare at the pages unread,
After the long day's whirl.

After I steal out at dawn's first gleam,
After breaking of bread,
After awaking from last faded dream,
After the first soft tread.

After I doze with mug brimming o'er,
After sweet voices in round,
After I watch each one out the door,
After each fading sound.

After I fell the first lonely fall,
After the smiling blue eyes,
After the moments brought to recall,
After each hour as it dies.

After the busy afternoon's flight,
After Orion looks down,
After the lights go on for the night,
After races in sleepers and gown.

After each tender one has climbed to my knee,
After each hug and smile,
After story of brave sailor and sea,
After more tumbling awhile.

After Mom has called each one to his bed,
After the quiet draws near,
After each sleepy face has long fled,
After I pray for each dear.

FACE TO FACE

By Boots Mayberry

I am and then
I shall be

at a twinkling
stepped into eternity.

In your sight
no more to be.

But you opened
at last to me.

I see as thou
imagined be.

O mortal!
Put on immortality!

The Mayberry family

A WORD FROM BOOTS

Dear Friends,

It was a time when boys became men and men became heroes or a memory in a blinding flash. The youth that I had would never be seen again. There were no young men returning from the battlefields—we were all old.

On our missions our aircraft left glistening contrails in the vivid sky, evidence that we had been there and gone away, leaving a part of ourselves. To quote from *Summer of '42,* "Life is made up of small comings and goings. And for everything we take with us, there is something we leave behind."

I pray that in my comings and goings I have left behind some comfort, hope, and the promise of a sunny tomorrow. I think of myself as a contrail, perhaps as evidence that I have walked among you.

Boots

ABOUT LINDA APPLE

 Linda is the author of *Writing Life ~ Your Stories Matter; Connect! ~ A Simple Guide to Public Speaking for Writers; POW Promises Kept, The Inspriring Stories of Boots Mayberry;* and *Women of Washington Avenue,* the first novel in her Moonlight Mississippi Series.

In addition to writing, Linda is a motivational speaker.

She lives in Northwest Arkansas with her husband, Neal. Their five children, five children-in-love, and ten grandchildren live close by.

More great books from Pen-L Publishing

**Coming
November 2014!**

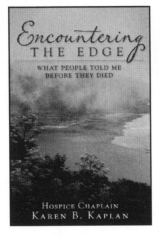

**Coming
November 2014**

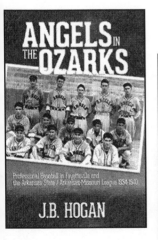

Visit Pen-L.com

Made in the USA
Charleston, SC
27 October 2014